Enjoy the Ride

Enjoy the Ride

Frank Daly

Edited by Karyn Dempsey

ISBN: 1507679432
ISBN 13: 9781507679432
Library of Congress Control Number: 2015901201
CreateSpace Independent Publishing Platform
North Charleston, South Carolina

This book is dedicated to all of you who ask questions with an open heart and mind.

Table of Contents

Acknowledgments

MY GRATITUDE AND love goes to my many loyal clients, who have continuously encouraged me to write this book and supported me over the years. I also owe a special debt of gratitude to Karyn Dempsey for helping me extend and refine my thinking and ultimately bring this book to fruition. I owe a debt of gratitude to my brother Terrence who helped me understand the constant expansion of life. I also acknowledge my parents, Frank and Kathy, and my sister Alice, who have consistently believed in me and encouraged me to push my limits. And finally, thanks to my son, Tristan, who will always be my greatest teacher.

Introduction

THIS BOOK IS an invitation to discover what you already know and to understand the transformative power you possess to create whatever you desire. The teachings here are not new; in fact, these things have been said many times, echoing through history as a constant reminder that all you could ever want or be you already have and are.

The key is remembering what you understand on a cellular level. This innate information comes to you in pieces as needed relative to what you experience in the moment, in the same way a GPS works, revealing one turn at a time at precisely the time it is needed. If you trust that the directions being provided are correct, you will act on the instruction and make your way safely to your destination with relative ease. As you read this book, you will realign with your own personal navigation system (your higher self), your own internal guidance system that is there all the time to navigate you in any direction you choose. If you do not trust in this system, you will take action that moves you away from your desired location, and often, frustration, anger, and despair will follow; however, as these ideas will demonstrate, the driving engine in navigating through your human experience is centered on your beliefs. Investigating your belief system and determining whether those beliefs are serving or hindering you is part of the journey of this book, and you will be offered straightforward, practical techniques that will immediately affect your life.

This book is not intended to be read quickly or in large doses. It is suggested that you pause where indicated and contemplate the application of these ideas to your daily living. As you read, you will gain a sense of already knowing what is being revealed, and the journey of self-expansion will continue far beyond the final pages.

As we gather to explore this endeavor we call life
Raising a glass to cheer the road that lies unknown
With a whisper from a wiser, hold no expectation
So our true self will be revealed for then we can
Dance in harmony with our most
important relationship
Self!

CHAPTER 1

Imagination Creates Reality

"The true journey of discovery consists not in seeking new landscapes but in having fresh eyes."

MARCEL PROUST

THE WAY IT works is very simple but the implications are immense: all of your beliefs are based on your thoughts, your thoughts dictate your actions, and your actions shape your life. Once this is not only understood intellectually but also realized at the most fundamental level, you can create anything, absolutely *anything*, you desire.

When you hold your attention on a specific thought for an extended period of time, it will become a belief. Thoughts can become habitual, and the longer you replay a thought in your mind, the more concrete it becomes for you and the more likely you are to attract events that confirm a belief that subsequently forms your reality. For example, imagine you meet someone you are attracted to. Despite your longing to be with this particular person, you find your affection is not returned and the person rejects you. As a result, you may find yourself experiencing a feeling of sadness, even loneliness. These feelings occur because of corresponding thoughts such as "I must have done something wrong" or "I must not be attractive enough."

These thoughts are a product of a belief that you need to be in a relationship to be happy or that if you do not find someone, you are going to be lonely for the rest of your life. If your originating belief was, "I am an incredible person. I know I deserve the best; I am fine on my own." Then the rejection would have no impact on your emotions whatsoever.

Thoughts create a vibration based on the belief attached to them. This vibration will generate a coresponding feeling which will indicate whether the belief is a product of your *higher mind* or your *thinking mind.*

What is the higher mind?

Your higher mind is pure positive energy. It goes by many names in many cultures: God, spirit, source, universal energy, and so forth. The higher mind is a divine awareness that you are born with and that never leaves you; it connects you to your true essence, your inner compass, your highest spiritual expression. Your higher mind is able to see the big picture and not get caught up in the worrisome details of the thinking mind.

Observe how you are feeling in this moment. Notice *you* are not that feeling; it is just a vibration the body is experiencing, produced by thoughts of the mind attached to your beliefs. It is the thought generated by a belief that creates the vibration. If the feeling resonates with self, in other words, if it makes you feel relaxed, satisfied, peaceful, and balanced, then bathe in that vibration. If the vibration is disruptive, diminishing, negative, know this is telling you the belief is out of alignment with your higher mind and it is time to dismantle that belief.

How do we identify information emanating from the higher mind?

If you feel good, you are following your higher mind, and this is the easiest and surest way to know you are heading in the direction of your desires. When you experience thinking-level emotions, such as guilt, fear, self-doubt, and anger, or simply a gut feeling that something is not right for you, this is an indication that you have moved away from your higher mind. It is the thinking mind that will labor over a problem or cling to a story or a self-defeating habit. The job of the thinking mind is to perceive what the higher mind conceived. The thinking mind only knows what has happened, what is concrete and tangible. Most people give the thinking mind too much responsibility and, oftentimes, too much power to control the decision-making process.

You have the ability to access your higher mind at any time, to find wisdom in your chaos, a purpose in your challenges. You do not need to take a class, study a philosophy, or learn a new system because you already have built into you all you need to find your true path.

Think about how a GPS system works. The GPS is the higher mind. Its job is to understand the big picture and consequently navigate to your destination using the path of least resistance. For example, if you want to go to San Diego and you live in Phoenix, you likely have some past experience that allows you to predict what the journey entails; at the very least, you know you will be heading west. You place the coordinates into the GPS, and the first thing it tells you is to head south from your current destination. If the thinking mind tries to take over at this point, you will question, "How does south get me west?" But if you just allow and follow the directions and know that the system will work and ultimately lead you in the right direction, you can relax, knowing that eventually the path will turn west.

The thinking mind gets you into trouble when you question how south can eventually get you west. You doubt, question, worry, and stew over the details and become stuck, unable to move in any direction at all. The thinking mind does not have the capacity to see the bigger picture. You must allow and trust that the higher mind will lead you in the direction you need to go and that it will never steer you off course.

When you keep your focus on the vibration dictated by the higher mind, all you need to do is act on those thoughts, even if they do not make sense to the thinking mind at the time. Know that these actions, these ideas that resonate with you, will eventually lead you where you need to go. This is your inner guiding system that is with you at all times and will never leave you. Your only real job is to feel good, experience the positive vibration of the inspired thoughts of the higher mind, and then simply act on those thoughts. And at the times when you do not feel good, do not judge yourself. Just know that it is all simply a part of the process, such as when the GPS tells you take a U-turn; you simply slow down and do so, no harm done.

How do we create our own reality through our thoughts?

Think about how a movie screen works. Upon the screen are the images of a story you call a movie, but where are the images you see actually coming from? They are coming from the projector, of course. The point I am making is that *you* are the projector of all things you see. The projector doesn't take cues from the screen. The screen is merely a reflection of what the projector is projecting upon the screen. Human beings are ultimately projectors, but you forget this transformative power you possess. Because you are this complex projector of your experience, everything you see on the outside world is created by the thoughts you give your attention to. Just like an individual frame that passes in front of the projector's light, a thought you hold creates a vibrational frequency, which then is reflected to the outside world. Your work is to become conscious of your vibration. Your feelings are the indicators of where you are vibrationally. If you like how you feel, continue, and more of the same will arrive to match this vibration. If you do not like the experience, change your vibration, and you will change your experience. You are always in control of the movie you see.

How can we keep our vibration tuned to our higher awareness?

There are many different ways to keep your vibration tuned to your higher awareness, but it is important to know that the method is just a focal point, allowing you to vibrate at a higher frequency. You must pick the way that resonates with you and simply surrender to the feeling. This is why humans have been engaged in ritual behavior since the dawn of time; however, it is not merely the practice that provides the shift. Alignment happens due to the vibrational shift that occurs during the process.

It has often been stated that all roads lead to happiness. When phrases like this come up, most of the time they are overlooked or misunderstood. When you look closely at this statement, though, you will find it is absolutely true. The truth is found when you understand the definition of happiness. Happiness is a state of being that has nothing to do with the outside reality you created for your experience. You often attach an experience as a reason for the happiness; for example, you might look back and remember being happy on vacation or with someone you love. You might imagine you will be happy in the future when you reach a goal or obtain a material item you desire. The truth is that none of these things has the power to make you happy. It is your state of being in a particular moment that is the true happiness. Therefore, it is possible to experience happiness at any time and in any moment, regardless of your external experience.

Is it possible to detach from external circumstances so completely that you can remain happy even if something truly unpleasant is occurring in your life?

Yes! The next time an event occurs that triggers a negative feeling, take a moment to investigate why you feel the way you do. It is in that moment that you have the ability to wake up from the dream and tell yourself it is not real and that you have become disconnected from your higher mind. The feeling in your body will subside once you realize that the belief is a choice you are making. You have the power to make a new choice.

Nothing in life has meaning outside of the meaning you give it. If someone criticizes you and you have a belief that they are right you will feel bad. Again, this is a choice. Why do you give your power away and let others determine your well-being? You are the only one who can determine your wellness.

This book is about the fact that you have the ability to create your own beliefs. Why not create beliefs that resonate with your higher self, that make you feel good, and that allow you to enjoy your life to the fullest? If you go into your day believing that you have the ability to feel 100 percent happy, you have a much better chance of actually feeling that way.

What if you are in a situation where you feel that you should not change your belief because your belief is that you are being wronged and you should not allow someone to treat you in such a way?

If you see yourself as a victim, you will be abused. If your belief is that you are not a victim, your external conditions will change because your vibration no longer makes you a cooperative component of that circumstance. Was there ever a time when you felt helpless but then changed your belief? The actions of those around you will change, too, as you see yourself differently.

You can really only be hurt or affected if you actually believe the insult on some level. If you are told you are stupid, for example, this would have no effect on you if no part of you bought into that belief. If it did not affect you, you would continue to maintain your higher vibration, and there would not be a problem. Once you change your beliefs, it is important to know that the people in your life may do one of several things: they may grow, they make changes in their own behavior accordingly, or they may leave your life, unable to adjust to your new belief system. Whichever they choose, you are no longer trapped in negativity, a thinking vibration where you are buying into a belief that does not feel good and that pulls you away from your higher mind.

Know that when you do feel the pain or frustration of a negative emotion, you did not do anything wrong. See it as a good thing, a reminder, a sign that this is an area to work on, and an opportunity to grow. This is what you are here on this earth for, to understand the contrast that is your life, to wake up from the illusion. You can never feel the glory of worthiness if you have never felt the pain of unworthiness. Be compassionate toward yourself in these times, and know that you are being directed on a path to your higher mind.

The abounding life one possesses
Eludes itself if unknown to what is abundance
Not to be taken from another
For only wreckage will be found
Discovery is ours to obtain its true value
Far below the current to the quiet depths
Where treasures are revealed
Now open the chest
For Love will abound

CHAPTER 2

Abundance of Love

"If you are pained by any external thing, it
is your judgment of this
thing which pains you, and it is in your
power to wipe out that judgment now."

MARCUS AURELIUS

THE PEOPLE WHOM you draw into your life are a direct reflection of how you see the world and yourself. Because like attracts like, looking closely at the people you have brought into your life can tell you a great deal about your own beliefs.

Your self-perception creates a vibrational frequency that will attract a similar vibration in another person or circumstance. You are always in a state of telling a story in your mind about who you are, and that story sets off a vibrational frequency that will dictate what you bring to your life. The following story is an example.

Ever since Sam Martin was a young boy, his father would always tell him that the Martins were a lucky family. "It is the darndest thing," his father would explain. "Things just work out for us." Sam recalls that, when his father would pull into a busy parking lot with no spaces available, he would cheerfully announce, "Don't worry; there is always a place up front for the Martins." And sure enough, his father would always find a parking spot. When Sam worried about his ability to make the high-school baseball team, his father reminded him, "The Martins are lucky, son. If it is what you want, it is what you will get." Sam's father was always right; things just seemed to work out for him because he was a Martin.

As Sam grew older, he of course realized that things do not always go your way in life. But the story he tells himself, the core of his belief, is that he is a fortunate person and things "just work out for him." Because of this core belief, he not only attracts more positive outcomes in his life, but he is also less dismayed when things do not materialize as he desires, for in the back of his mind he believes that eventually things will go his way.

The story you tell yourself about yourself will dictate the outcome of your life.

If you tell yourself a story that includes the belief that you are not a good person, that you do not deserve love, that true love is rare and hard to find, that relationships never really last, you will continue to attract these experiences in your life. Remember, you are the projector of the outside world, so if you consistently use your thoughts to project an image of yourself as a person who is lonely, you will perpetuate this reality.

Wherever you are and whatever you are attracting in your life this very moment is a direct reflection of your vibrational frequency. There is no past, only your vibrational thoughts thinking about the past and consequently creating your present reality. The past and future are illusions. Your past does not equal your future unless you allow it to. Every moment is a new moment to create, to think new or different thoughts. Allow this idea to fully sink in—at any moment you can change the story you tell yourself about yourself; at any moment you can change your life. You are today where your thoughts have brought you; you will be tomorrow where your thoughts take you.

What about circumstances that seem out of your control? Aren't there some things that happen to us that really have nothing to do with our "story"?

What you have control over is your perception, not the external circumstance. That perception is what creates a vibrational frequency and what will direct what you are experiencing now. While you consciously did not invite the situation, you cannot experience something you did not vibrationally agree to. Everything is ultimately in your control. If you respond differently to external circumstances, they will change. There is a profound difference between reacting and responding. When you react, you are denying the present moment; you are trying to force external circumstances to be what you want them to be. When you respond, you are more open, more positive about the possible outcome of a situation. So, if you respond, you create a positive outcome; if you react, you create a negative outcome. Nothing in life has a built-in meaning; you give it meaning, and at that moment you have the ability to choose positive or negative, response or reaction.

As this applies to love, if you want love, you must become that which you desire. Whatever it is that you want from a relationship in your life, be that on your own first. Although it may be hard to understand when you are feeling lonely, it is not the external relationship that you are craving but the feeling you have when you are in that relationship. You do not attract what you want; you attract what you feel from within. Place your attention on the feeling you wish to create and recognize that you are complete on your own. Every subject has two sides, the wanting and the lack. This is where it is easy to go awry. Are you focusing on wanting or on lacking?

Your imagination will always precede that which you create in your life. When you feel lonely or isolated, it is possible to imagine yourself as happy and fulfilled. Focus on the vibration that arises in your body when you see yourself in a loving relationship that meets your needs and allows you to expand. What you focus your attention on will grow and will be attracted to you.

Most people have bought into a reality that says if you are sitting at home on a Saturday night with no one to call or nothing to do, you must be lonely. However, isn't it possible to be surrounded by people at a noisy nightclub and still feel alone? That experience demonstrates that the feeling of loneliness is something that comes from within and is based on your thoughts and perceptions, not on the external world. It is perception that creates reality.

If your belief is that you are a lonely person, then it will not matter what your external world looks like; the feeling will persist. When you are in a positive state of mind, everything in the physical world will become illuminated; therefore, do whatever you must to get to that higher state of feeling, and all that you want—whether it is love, money, or something else—will arrive. Get a good feeling first. Focusing on lack will bring more lack, while feeling good brings more things that feel good—including love.

You get to decide, in every moment, how to perceive your life. It is possible for you to stop a belief, interrupt a thought process, and live your life differently. Once your belief changes, your thoughts change, and once your thoughts change, your actions will change.

Most people tend to see the essential process backward. They believe that once they are in a loving and fulfilling relationship, they will be happy. But it actually works the opposite way. You must feel the change within, and then your focus will change and the external world will follow. Whatever you are feeling, you will attract more of the same; the way to create a fundamental change in your life is to feel it differently.

The next time you are feeling lonely, is it possible to just accept it? Society often portrays being alone as something sad and pitiable, definitely a situation to be avoided. It is possible to stop fighting against the feeling, though, and allow yourself to live with the discomfort. Begin by letting go of any judgment you have regarding your status. Fully accept where you are, without an inner voice evaluating or analyzing it. Do not compare yourself to others, as this only leads to self-criticism. Comparison is a dysfunction, as no two things are ever the same.

Distract yourself from your self-judgment and negativity by identifying a part of your life that makes you feel good. Reflect on this aspect, imagining the details so thoroughly that you begin to feel your vibration change, shifting to a more positive state of mind. Once you are in this state, do not allow the negative thoughts to pull you back down. When they arise within you, resist and return to the place that makes you feel good.

Surrender the idea of *how* it is supposed to happen, and focus on the feeling you want to happen. It is easy to get stuck believing that a particular sequence of events must occur before you will get what you want. Modern culture teaches that it is necessary to go to a bar, get out and socialize, try online dating, and so forth in order to "find" someone. Use the idea of how it is supposed to look only to generate the feeling you wish to obtain, and then drop the prescribed process and dwell only in the feeling. If you are fixated on love coming in only a predictable way or looking a certain way, you may miss what is right in front of you.

Again, it is the thinking mind that wants to take over and find a rational way that the relationship will occur. Drop that and trust that the organizing principles of the universe will guide you to what is best in order to create the reality you desire. When you do this, you will begin acting on your inspiration rather than going through the motions of what you think should happen. When you feel the urge to act on something, that impulse represents the organizing principles at work. Do not question how it is going get you where you want to go; just trust that you will not be misled. This is response, not reaction. You will no longer be restricted by what other people believe must happen, but instead tuned to your own internal guiding system, which will never steer you in the wrong direction. Just as with a GPS, you put in the coordinates of your desired destination and then know that you will get there. Set your vibrational frequency, and then let go, knowing that, step by step, you will be given the instructions you need, even if there is a turn or two you do not understand.

Trust that in each moment, you know exactly what you need to know to get to the next step. Recognizing the feeling you generate based on your imagination is all that needs to be done to obtain your desire. The desire inspires an action, and inspirationed action is effortless. If it requires effort, it is not the right action to make at that time. Again, this is response, not reaction. When you react, you are telling the universe this shouldn't be and fighting against what is; responding, conversely, is accepting what is happening and perceiving it in a way that works for you and allows you to be positive rather than negative.

Why does the euphoric feeling of new love fade?

New love seems to fade because you think it is the other person that made you feel the euphoric feeling. But it is never the other person. He or she is merely a catalyst, a trigger for what already exists inside of you. When you are in love, it is *you* that made you feel that way. When you think it is the other person, you will get angry with him or her and disenchanted in the relationship because you thought it was the other person from the beginning—but it never was. You hold him or her responsible for how you feel, but it isn't his or her responsibility to make you feel good. It is your responsibility to stay at your high vibration.

So you move on, hoping to recapture that euphoria, but again (and here is where the pattern of perpetual dissatisfaction begins), it will fade. As long as you continue to believe your fulfillment is outside of yourself, you will be caught in a trap of continual disappointment. Remember, you are the projector creating your reality.

Imagine you are watching a movie projected on a screen, and you see a scene you do not like and that does not feel as if it fits with the story. You wouldn't get up from your seat and attack the screen, ripping it down to make the scene go away. You would go to the projection room and edit the film, making the necessary changes before sitting back down to enjoy the movie. If you rip the screen to shreds, the projector will continue, the image will still appear. You need to go back and change the film. This is what you need to do in regard to the external world. When experiencing something you do not like, instead of continuing to wonder why the picture is not appealing, examine your thoughts (the projector), the ones that created the external image in the first place.

If your thought pattern is an automatic focus on what you do not have, you will feel a sense of lack and only attract more lack into your life. If you pay deliberate attention to your thoughts and use them to create a feeling of joy, love, and gratitude for what you have in life right now, you will attract more of the same.

Upon arrival into this play
A character is formed
Molded by those who appear familiar.
If clay is my structure
Will I ever be permitted to use my own hands?
Are we Destin to handle this on our own?
We are our own due to family
Obligation isn't its design
Just familiarity so we feel at home.

CHAPTER 3

Prosperity

"Prosperity is to have the ability to do what you want to do when you want to do it."

BASHAR

You CAN ATTRACT prosperity and wealth into your life the same way you attract love or anything else you desire—by becoming that which you seek. If you define yourself as prosperous and feel a sense of abundance in your life, you will inevitably attract more of the same. Once again, you must examine your beliefs and consider how they support your thoughts, this time in regard to money. Do you have a core belief that money only comes from hard work, only if you are well educated, or only if you deserve it on some level?

If you are deeply invested in seeing yourself as a person in a state of lack and find yourself always focusing on the things you do not have or how your life can and should be better, this belief will become a core part of your identity; you will only attract more lack into your life.

Your thoughts will propel you to perform both large and small actions that will keep you stuck. Additionally, you will view the world with a biased filter, only recognizing aspects of your world that confirm your belief. All of this will keep you in a rut, running the same path over and over again. You must stop focusing on what you do not want and shift your attention to that which you desire.

How can you shift your focus when you can't even pay your bills?

If you cannot pay your bills or buy the basic necessities you need to provide for yourself and your family, you can easily become overwhelmed by a sense of deficiency, and the attached negative emotions will consume your focus and lower your vibration. From this place, it can be challenging to feel a sense of abundance, to define yourself differently. It may require a great deal of mental self-discipline; however, rather than allowing yourself to dwell on the negative aspects of your financial situation, as best you can, strive to shift your focus and find a place in your life that feels good. This can seem difficult when you are deeply enveloped in a negative or depressed space, so begin if you must with something small—a sunset, a flower, the laughter of a child, a poem, a piece of music, a good meal, anything you can use to distract yourself from your feelings of lack and raise yourself to a higher vibration.

Remember, this is a process. Do not expect to be able to go from despair to joy immediately. The shift to a higher vibration is accomplished by taking small steps in a new direction. If you found yourself going one hundred miles per hour, speeding in the wrong direction, you would not make a sudden and sharp turn in the opposite direction. The result of such a move would be disastrous. Instead, you slow down, take your foot off the gas, find an off-ramp, and look for ways to decelerate in order to make a smooth turn. If you could not find any way to slow down, the car would eventually run out of gas and bring you to a stop, but this is, of course, the long route. In other words, if you are in a depressed state, eventually the energy will exhaust you. It will loosen and shift in some way, and you will consequently change your focus, even if it is only for a short time. However, this brief relief represents a crucial moment, providing a window of opportunity to begin to slow things down and make new choices that will eventually turn you in a new direction.

It is impossible to clearly recognize your options while you are in a negative space, trapped in a lower frequency. Once outside of this trap, though, you begin to understand that there are many ways you can view any given situation in your life. This is what is considered "thinking outside the box"; actually, you are observing from outside the box when you begin to see yourself from an objective perspective.

When you stand outside of yourself and simply witness what you are feeling, you will see your emotional response as a choice you are making and be able to evaluate whether this choice is serving you well or causing you more pain. This is not to avoid the reality of your situation, but to raise your vibration and get yourself to a place of clarity. Higher-vibration feelings will bring a deeper understanding to all areas of your life.

Isn't it irresponsible to ignore your negative financial state?

You do not ignore your financial state, but begin to understand that your beliefs about money and your relationship with money are what created your financial situation in the first place.

Why is it that you desire more money? Most likely, it is so that you can have certain experiences that you believe will increase your level of happiness in life (more choices, less work, more material possessions, etc.). Society teaches that money, health, and love are the essential things necessary to be happy. These are not separate; they are all a product of being in tune with your higher mind, corresponding to your higher vibration. Money is a part of your experience, but it's not your only experience; it is not the lone way to get the things that you desire. An example of this principle is demonstrated in the story of the fisherman and the businessman:

The businessman was at the pier of a small coastal Mexican village when a small boat with just one fisherman docked. Inside the boat were several large yellowfin tuna. The businessman complimented the fisherman on the quality of his fish and asked how long it took to catch them. The fisherman replied only a little while.

The businessman then asked why he didn't stay out longer and catch more fish. The fisherman said he had enough to support his family's immediate needs. The businessman then asked, "But what do you do with the rest of your time?"

The fisherman said, "I sleep late; fish a little; play with my children; take a siesta with my wife, Maria; and stroll into the village each evening where I sip wine and play guitar with my amigos. I have a full and busy life, señor."

The businessman scoffed. "I am a Harvard MBA, and I could help you. You should spend more time fishing and with the proceeds buy a bigger boat. With the proceeds from the bigger boat, you could buy several boats; eventually you would have a fleet of fishing boats. Instead of selling your catch to a middleman, you would sell directly to the processor and eventually open your own cannery. You would control the product, processing, and distribution. You would need to leave this small coastal fishing village and move to Mexico City, LA, and eventually New York City, where you would run your expanding enterprise."

The fisherman asked, "But señor, how long will this all take?"

To which the businessman replied, "Fifteen to twenty years."

"But what then, señor?"

The businessman laughed and said, "That's the best part! When the time is right, you would announce an IPO and sell your company stock to the public and become very rich. You would make millions."

"Millions, señor? Then what?"

The businessman said, "Then you would retire and move to a small coastal fishing village, where you would sleep late, fish a little, play with your kids, take a siesta with your wife, and stroll to the village in the evenings where you could sip wine and play your guitar with your amigos."

The fisherman, still smiling, looked up and said, "Isn't that what I'm doing right now?"

—Author Unknown

This parable demonstrates that increased cash flow is not the only route to obtaining that which you desire, because what is desired is not necessarily money itself but the experience, the state of mind that you believe having more money will provide. Focus on what you want to experience, and then the money may show up, or some other avenue will open and allow you to create the desired outcome. If you are just focused on the money, then you are limiting the ways in which the universe can bring you your experience.

Have you ever noticed that when you are feeling good, everything flows well for you? When you are in a good mood, the world seems to cooperate; the traffic lights turn green, people are friendlier, you receive generous compliments, and life just seems to go your way. You are not happy because things are working out; things are working out because you are happy. The reason good things are happening is that you did not hold any conditions; you did not strive to control outside aspects. Notice that it is when you try to control external circumstances that things do not flow.

Again, let go of how you think it is supposed to look. When you hold onto a rigid process, you limit the infinite scenarios and situations that can bring you what you desire. Remember, once the endpoint is in the GPS, you only have to pay attention to how you feel when you make a decision or commit to an action. Trust your internal navigation, and you will be led to your destination.

If you are listening to a country station and waiting for a rock song to be played, you will be waiting forever. You must change the frequency on the dial to get to the song you want to hear. If you are in a lower vibration, feeling negative emotions such as guilt, fear, shame, or lack, you cannot reach a state of getting what you desire. You must first "change the station" and tune your vibration to a higher frequency. Once you are at this higher frequency, you will hear what you want to hear and recognize the myriad of creative ways to manifest that which you desire.

Can you imagine yourself winning the lottery and living in a mansion? Picture what it looks like and feels like when you are there, what you see when you look out the window or open the door. Sense it fully, as if it has already happened. Then drop all expectations of *how* it is going to come into your life, and just act on your highest joy without questioning.

When you are in a state of joy and a desire arises, it cannot be wrong because you are following your inner GPS, which knows where you should be. If you stop and question it, you are questioning the process itself, doubting the GPS of how going south can get you west. This doubt is the thinking mind trying to rationalize your actions. The misunderstanding comes from the thinking mind, but the path to your desire, the turns and choices you must make, come from your higher mind. Doubt freezes your actions and keeps you from getting to your goal. Until you trust and drop judgment, you cannot get to where you want go.

Often the source of interference comes from erroneous judgment, from not trusting the GPS system and comparing your situation to past experiences or asking others what they think. Often others will confirm your doubts, keeping you stuck in your negative beliefs, in your repetitive patterns of dysfunction. They do this not to hold you back; it is because they are in a different place and cannot see the path from your point of view.

What determines success?

There are many stories about people who were at the top of their class, went to the best schools, and worked hard their entire lives, yet never experienced prosperity or a sense of abundance. In other instances, there are those who earned mediocre grades in school or did not attend school at all, who were deemed "lazy" by society, and yet became leaders in their chosen fields. While arguably some people will enjoy a better all-around educational experience, the bottom line is that *you* are ultimately responsible for your success or failure, both in business and in your personal life. It's all about what *you* create, how you talk to yourself, how you see yourself in the world based on your beliefs. The person who goes to school, earns a graduate degree, and cannot get a job wonders why the high-school dropout is wealthy. The degree is not what creates the prosperity; the belief that the degree is needed in order to obtain success creates the prosperity. Conversely, if you do not think that a degree is needed to prosper in life, then this becomes your reality.

The collective society creates a condition that dictates you cannot be successful unless you follow a socially approved process. This is taught over and over, as all students are placed in the same standardized-testing box and taught one path as the road to a successful and happy life. How disappointing it must be for young adults to go through the prescribed routine and follow all the rules, only to finally "arrive" at a feeling of emptiness and scarcity. Conditions should never be standardized with a one-size-fits-all approach because there are millions of ways to reach the same objective, and the path can never be the same for two people. While the ultimate goal is the same for everyone—to reach a higher vibration—the path that leads each person to this place will be different.

It is not in your best interest to try to figure out what success is through others. Others may be used as an example ("if they can do it, so can I"), but the way they go about it may very well be different from your path.

The thinking mind is trying to conceive through seeing someone else. These examples are only to demonstrate a vibrational frequency that you can aspire to match, yet you can never travel someone else's road. It is impossible. It would better serve you to define what you believe to be success at this moment in your life, focus on that energy, and act on what comes to mind as a product of that vibration. Your definition of success will then become your own; it will change to what fits you. The only constant is change, and what changes are your perceptions. This is the very essence of free will.

A simple shuttering of the eyes
To what is
Awakens us to a vision
Exploration of the universe becomes boundless
Holding no contempt for where we are
Directing us to what is possible
Observation does not make a believer
Believing gives us something to observe
Clean the lens for this grand vision
When understood
Imagination will excel this joyous ride

CHAPTER 4

Illusions

*"Reality is merely an illusion,
albeit a very persistent one."*

ALBERT EINSTEIN

Everything you see in your physical reality is letting you know what vibrational frequency you are at in the moment. When you fully understand this, it will serve you greatly, for you will no longer look at the external circumstances of your life with judgment. Instead, you can simply observe your surroundings and interpret what they are telling you about how your thoughts are currently operating. When you see your reality as a mirror of your dominant thoughts, any rigidity in your mental labeling of positive and negative will begin to soften into simple categories—preference or nonpreference. You can no longer blame your circumstances for your unhappiness or discomfort, for you will realize that it is your own thought vibration that is producing such circumstances and that you have the freedom, in every moment, to change your thoughts and consequently change your reality. When observing from this perspective—preference or nonpreference—you have the ability to move more fluidly through your life. You will understand that the universe operates on your behalf; it always has, but now you will see it.

It is easy to blame others for the things in your life that are not working. You may think it is the actions of a friend, a family member, a boss, or others that have brought an undesirable situation into your life. However, when you examine how your thoughts have created this judgment, you will realize that blame is unnecessary.

While it is important not to hold others accountable for your life circumstances, it is also important not to blame yourself for discomfort. When you notice that you are stuck in negativity, acknowledge your thoughts and see them as just that—simply thoughts. In this moment, you *break the pattern of identifying with your patterned thoughts* and make room for a new choice.

It is equally disruptive to your process to compare yourself with others and become angry, jealous, or frustrated with your situation rather than exercising patience with yourself. The game of comparison is truly a trap, and it is one that is especially hard to avoid in a capitalistic society that thrives on you believing in your lack—that is, if you make such and such a purchase, you can fill this void and somehow be more worthy or happier. As you have probably experienced, this feeling, this kind of "happy," is short-lived, and you soon find yourself waiting for the next time you can temporarily satisfy your endless sense of lack.

At the heart of this stress is the tendency to compare yourself with others rather than focus on your own experience. If everyone around you had the same things as you, you would not feel inferior or superior. It is only when you compare what you have to what others have that you come out feeling different—either insufficient or abundant. When you compete with another, you create an internal struggle. Why do you need to feel better or more important than others? How much better do you have to be before you will allow yourself to be satisfied, before you can finally rest? How long can you maintain this level of satisfaction before the feeling of lack again creeps up in your mind? When caught in this endless cycle, you will never have enough. You will never be wholly satisfied with what you have, for you believe that your happiness comes from "winning" or "having" rather than simply being. If you believe the only thing that will bring you good feelings is the outcome of a situation, you forget the value of the journey.

It is a false assumption to think that those with more information or stuff are somehow better off. You manifest what you need at a particular moment in time in order to get to where you need to be. If you are in New York City and need to get to Los Angeles, you would need more information than if you were in San Diego and needed to get to Los Angeles. Having more is not always better; having more information might sometimes simply be necessary, but only based specifically on where you are and where you need to go.

It is often said that the beauty of life is in the journey. Yet you cannot truly understand the wisdom of these words until you have acquired something you desperately desired, something you believed would make you happy at last, only to find that it is empty. The feeling dissipates, and you realize that ultimately material items have no ability to bring you a sense of lasting contentment.

The irony of this endless cycle is that when you re-direct your attention and focus on the process, the goal is reached automatically. It may not look exactly like what you imagined, but the vibrational feeling in your body will be a perfect match. So rather than competing with others, and racing to a finish line, act on the individual pieces of information as they are presented and do not worry about the ultimate outcome. Remain in a state of collaboration because you are all working toward the same goal, which is peace and harmony. The more you collaborate with others, the better you will feel, and these good-feeling vibrations will create consequences even greater than you imagined. A fundamental sense of well-being is derived from working with others, feeling a part of a community, and sharing a common goal.

How can you escape the constant feeling of unworthiness?

Fear, doubt, and a sense of unworthiness are quiet culprits that can lead to frustration, anxiety, and even depression. One of the surest ways to cut yourself off from obtaining your desires is to perpetuate a feeling of unworthiness. The very fact that you exist is proof that you are worthy. When you are caught in a downward spiral of self-loathing, a small but important shift will occur when you simply pause and fully recognize what you are feeling. When you shift your awareness and look directly into your own sorrow, you can begin to recognize the belief that has taken hold of you and to remember that you can choose a different belief. So, rather than fight the feeling, you walk straight toward it. As you recognize that the fuel behind the feeling is simply a mental story you have created, a phantom, the feeling of unworthiness will begin to dissipate.

No one person in this world is more important or less important than any other. Can you take two pieces out of a puzzle and determine which one is the more valuable? This is ridiculous, as both are needed to complete the picture. Without either, "wholeness" cannot exist. Everything, from intellect to materialism, has set false standards in this world that must be met. This judgment is something many carry with them every day, not realizing it is all an illusion.

One of the reasons you do not pursue your dreams is that, at your core, there is a belief that you are not worthy of success. If you never pursue the goal, then you never have to find out that you are not worthy. That is a safety mechanism, keeping you from confronting the true possibilities of your life, keeping you safe and not risking the chance of recognizing your ultimate potential. The only possibility of becoming what you most want to be is to get out of your own way. But how do you do this? How do you get out of your own way? It begins by realizing that the world is full of possibilities.

If you start with the belief structure that it is possible, you will open up a portal of information allowing you to feel it as well as recognize it. If you follow through on this vibration, this belief, it will lead you to the information you need to create life-altering transformation. The key is that it starts with a belief; from that belief all else will change.

How does it make you feel to hear that you are unique and that there is no one in the world exactly like you? It should make you feel quite special, but instead society often reinforces the idea that if you are not like everyone else, you are somehow inferior or inadequate. When you value uniqueness rather than social standards, you will be free from this trap, free to be self-guided but also collaborative. It sounds like a paradox, but it is one that creates complete liberation, based not on comparison but on each individual's unique contribution to the whole.

Consider the complexity of a perfect gourmet meal. Each individual spice contributes a distinctive flavor that contributes to the beauty of the whole. Without this diversity there would be no contrast and the dish would be bland and one-dimensional. It is only when each spice maintains its individuality that haromony is achieved.

Even when things are going well, however, there can be resistance. When you are going through an altitude change, there is a transitional period that you must pass through. This may create the urge to descend; it is uncomfortable when you are not able to breathe as deeply. It is an unknowing state of being, but a necessary part of any transition. You think you know the best route, and usually it coincides with prescribed societal norms. However, once you recognize and accept that the route is out of your control and may be something you do not understand, you will be able to release the fear involved in this pain and move forward.

Trying to control what is going to happen creates pain. Instead of examining what is wrong, simply allow the experience to be what it is, even if it undesirable. Chances are good that you will be able to grow from its consequences and perhaps even be lifted to a higher altitude.

Imagine you are on vacation and you lose your wallet. You go through a panic. What could possibly be worse than losing your wallet so far from home? However, once you let go of the panic, allowing the experience to be what it is, you will not feel the pain. And once you truly accept the situation and distract yourself, you are able to see things clearly, rise above your panic, and find a solution, a new way to confront your problems. You cannot do this when you are locked inside your panic.

You can never see the entire puzzle; you can only see an individual piece. Trust that there is a process you cannot see, and you will be able to release your anxiety. Everything in this world is a piece of a puzzle, and your vibrational frequency will determine your ultimate picture. Once you pass through this state, you will realize transition was necessary to reach the new state. Do not panic. Do not think you must move back to where you are comfortable. Move forward to the new place, and trust that you will adapt to your growth.

How does the uncertainty principle relate to our experience?

In quantum physics, the uncertainty principle is a theory regarding the limits of how much can be predicted about the movement of quantum particles. How does this relate to you? The thinking mind cannot conceive all the variables that need to be in place in order for something to become an experience. There are way too many moving parts for you to see. But the higher mind, the superconscious mind, whatever name you would like to give it, can see everything. If you trust that your higher mind will lead, all you need to do is stay with the feelings you experience when visualizing yourself reaching your goal. Then, everything will be presented to you.

Nestled in the comfort of one's mind,
Inherited from nature,
The pure exhilaration life has to offer.
So how did we come to be lost in the woods?
After all, there is nothing more natural than a forest.
So why are we forsaken by the brush
Leaving us visually disabled?
A simple misunderstanding
that a clearing is all we need.

CHAPTER 5

Loving Life

"*Imagination is more important than knowledge. For knowledge is limited to all we now know and understand, while imagination embraces the entire world, and all there ever will be to know and understand.*"

ALBERT EINSTEIN

From the time you are very young you are taught that an examination of history will reveal a strategy for how to live well. If you conduct thorough research of the past, and collect enough data, you can confidently assert that you have the facts required in order to claim something is true, you have proof. If the majority of people find that a specific definition of truth reinforces their belief system, then confirmation bias takes over and history is solidified.

But why do you need to know the truth in the first place? Throughout history, it is apparent that people seem to need to believe that their story is the one true story and are unable to accept that a story might be a fiction and that the very tradition of historical scholarship does not reveal an eternal truth but the psychological needs of people at a particular moment in history with their own point to prove, or belief to reinforce. Historical narratives do not reveal any one clear direction or any final goal.

But still you persist. You try to pin everything down in order to gain some sort of elusive and definitive understanding of how you are to live your lives. You think that if you find this answer, your life will become easier, happier and more satisfying. Most of you believe that when you get what you desire that you are lucky. It is only luck if you do not understand how the universe operates. You will create the life you believe you deserve. If you feel you only deserve little, you will experience little, whereas if you have the expectation that life is abundant and you deserve the best, then the best is what you will experience. It all depends on the direction you choose, where you decide to focus your awareness. When Moses roamed the desert for forty years his followers were concerned with only having enough food and water to get through the day and believed that tomorrow they would surely be without. It was this concern that kept them lost. It wasn't until they trusted that what they needed would be there for them every day that they found the Promised Land, which was a place of abundance. Liberation can only be found when the feeling of lack is ceased.

There is not one right way to live. The beliefs you hold about life will create the conditions you experience. Consequently, if you are a survivalist you will experience life through a succession of circumstances that you must overcome, conversely, if you believe everything will always work out and do not concern yourself with the details of exactly how it is going to work out, you will experience an easy sense of flow in life. One way of living is not better than the other, just different and you can always choose which you prefer. You inherently have a built in mechanism that moves you in the path of least resistance and because of this you are always searching for an easier way to achieve what it is you desire. With this understanding, going from survival mode to a more relaxed mode allows you to transition easier.

If you can look at life as just one big experience like a novel, you realize that every situation and every character makes up that story and there isn't one character that is more important or less necessary than another. Superman is no better than Lex Luther because without the villain the hero could not fulfill his purpose. Everything that you experience is part of the story of life and from the infinite number of possibilities everyone has their own path to take, their own story to write.

So if this is the case, how can you write your story in a fashion of preferential desire? Simple: imagination.

When you talk about the imagination you often associate it with the creativity of an artist, whether it be a painter, musician, actor, etc. It is often believed that in order to be an accomplished artist one must have a superior imagination. This implies that there are people that have a limited imagination. Interestingly enough, whatever you believe will become your truth and the consequences of that belief will be witnessed in your world. When examined from the quantum state it becomes clear that an opinion, once professed, will harden into fact until such time when you choose to change your perspective and that fact devolves for another to solidify in its place. Imagination is what enables you to have the physical experience, if in alignment you will make it delightful.

Consider the well-known phrase, "Everything that is was once imagined." Imagination is at the core of your existence. Everything you experience was first imagined, or it would not come to fruition. The man living on the street had to first imagine himself doing so and after keeping this image in his thoughts long enough he created a strong belief that it could be possible to find himself homeless. Once this belief was solidified he pursued a series of actions based on the idea and the movement toward this determined destination began. The same holds true for the man living in a mansion. Regardless of the direction, the physics work the same. The universe does not discriminate. You imagine negative things when your thoughts are generated from a place of fear and lack. The emotion of fear has a frequency, much like frequency of a radio station. If you adjust the tuner on a radio to the frequency 99.7 you can only receive that particular program, whatever it may be. If you do not prefer that station, you must change the frequency in order to receive something different. You wouldn't try to reprogram 99.7 you would simply turn the dial to a new frequency. You experience fear when you hold the misunderstanding that you cannot change the station and shift in a new direction. Shifting is automatic, you are always adjusting. At times it might not feel like you are changing because you move to a similar frequency resulting in a similar outcome. When you examine fear you realize it is merely an indicator letting you know that where you are is not where you truly want to be. Facing your fear will help you move in a new direction and you will recognize that you are heading in the right direction when the fear dissipates and you feel a positive emotion such as joy, excitement, anticipation.

This is how your inner guidance system works, you ask for the destination and it guides you through your emotions in the same way a GPS works but instead of it telling you to make a right at the next intersection your inner guidance system nudges you with your emotions. Remaining aware of your emotions can make the ride much easier. The next time you experience a negative emotion realize it is telling you that it is time to recalculate. It does not matter how far off course you are it can still get you to your destination without fail, your job is to simply trust in it.

When you are fully conscious and aware of your inner self, you are able to create a belief that is in direct alignment with what you desire. This allows the imagination to work as a supportive collaborator as you become immersed in the feeling that results from your positive thoughts and beliefs. Although the physical reality may show no proof, the feelings generated will move you in a direction of your desires. Your actions will automatically align with these beliefs and the journey towards the physical begins.

Beliefs play a significant role. If you truly believe you can achieve what you have imagined, you will take actions in the direction of the desire with ease. All beliefs are valid, the thing to ask is are they working conjunction with what you would like to experience, if not, you can transform the belief so it works for you not against you. Again, it is not whether or not the belief is right or wrong but is it in alignment with what is desired.

When this concept is understood it becomes evident that all experiences appear about without judgment. Judgment will deny the discovery of the lesson needed to fully understand to get to the place of knowing how this all works. Remember removing characters from the story only confuses the reader it will never make it better.

You are constantly telling yourself a story about your life. Some people walk around with a story that tells them they are a victim, that nothing good ever happens to them. Some go through life with a success story, telling themselves that they are lucky and good things come their way. At any moment you can change your story, by changing your beliefs, and when beliefs change, life changes as well. Just like an actor who plays a part they have the ability to fit into a role by changing their concept of themselves. A great actor changes the concept of their character in order to tell the story. Simply believing they are another person allows the imagination to generate a new persona. The reason you marvel over this is because at your core you know that you too can change the concept of your character to one you desire.

After all, everything you experience is a fractal of how the universe works. In other words, you always create a reflection of what you already are in order to experience it in the physical world.

Once fully conscious of a belief it will become clear if the belief is beneficial or detrimental. Think of a belief like a moving vehicle, one that allows you to reach your destination. If you would like to get to Hawaii and your current location is Phoenix but the vehicle you possess is a car it would be nearly impossible to travel to your destination. There is nothing wrong with a car, but it is not beneficial if your goal is to travel across an ocean. The same is true for beliefs. None are inherently wrong, they are just sometimes out of alignment with a desire. So if you truly want to travel to Hawaii you are going to have to choose a different mode of transportation. Look carefully at your own desired destination and examine if you have beliefs that actually work against accomplishing that goal. Keep in mind that any desire you have in the first place can be experienced or you would not have the ability to imagine it.

It is time to transition to another belief when the one you are holding onto is not in sync with your higher self. This is similar to the feeling of eating a large meal. You start out hungry and if you are conscious you will know when your body is satisfied. If you are not conscious, your body will let you know when it is time to stop through the discomfort of overeating. When conscious, you remain balanced through the shift from one belief to another in order to get you to where it is you desire to go. In other words, if you are in Arizona and you believe heading east will get you to San Diego, at some point you will have to change direction to reach your destination. The further you proceed in the opposite direction the more effort it will take to get back in balance. The feeling of effort will keep you out of balance until a complete collapse of your system. This collapse is different for everyone and will also be different for the individual at different moments.

As you come to understand this structure of how beliefs work, you will find yourself with beliefs that create an effortless and enjoyable journey. Understand that the belief is the vehicle you utilize to take us to your destination. When you choose the vehicle that is most pleasurable in the moment you know without doubt it will provide the synchronistic journey needed to reach your destination.

A tiny ripple shows me this is a mere reflection
Wipping the slate clean
Leaving only what I intend to experience
As the pond settles
Only a smile remains

CHAPTER 6

Reflections

"Ignorance is our deepest secret."

BY SHANIYA PLUNKETT

As YOU SIT and consider all that you have understood from reading this book, notice how you are feeling. Your feelings are always an indicator of the direction you are moving in so remember, if you are not feeling good, you are not moving in the direction of your desire. Holding onto good feelings will always lead you in the direction that will bring you what you want in life. The same holds true for negative feelings which is the reason they feel bad. Again, they are an indicator of your direction so if you do not feel good you know it is time to change your course. Whether you are feeling positive or negative emotions, your inner guidance system is always at work. When you come to truly understand and trust this consistent inner mechanism you will always have a foundation to draw from. When worry or stress does arise in your life you will simply distract yourself with something that helps you to return to a state of feeling good and know that all will be well.

From this point forward, be conscious of the state of your feelings and more attune to these inner emotions than you are of the conditions or circumstances of your external world. When you need to make a decision, focus your attention on getting to a good feeling place and then make the decision or take action. When you are coming from a good feeling place the action you take will automatically move you in the direction of more good feelings. After all, your true desire is to feel good. People, places and situations are just expressions of your state of being which will always reflect back to you what is happening in your inner world. No matter what direction you go you will always be supported in the state you hold onto. If you believe you can achieve something you generate a feeling which will in return provide you with a course of action to take to reinforce that belief. Each step will unfold before you with ease. If you fully trust this system you will effortlessly enjoy the ride.

A good example of the results of this practice came when I was assisting a woman with use of her inner guidance system and manifesting her deepest desire: a loving and lasting relationship. She sat down and wrote in great detail what she wanted in her perfect mate and by getting specific in the details it helped her generate a feeling as if it he was already a part of her reality. She wrote down things such as how he greeted her every time they interacted, his smile as he gazed into her eyes, his ability to stay positive no matter what conflicts they confronted, and his ability to create abundance in their life together. After writing the letter she placed it in a book she had been reading and returned the book to her bookshelf. She would occasionally pull it out to read when she was feeling doubt but after a while of relying on the letter to make her feel good it started to have the opposite effect, it reminded her of the absence of it.

She came to me with her dilemma and I suggested she store the letter away, explained to her the purpose for the letter was to look beyond what is, in order to generate the feeling to allow her to be receptive to what essentially already exists. As she began to understand this more and more she would focus on things in her life that were already working with ease. She came to the conclusion that it wasn't a man, or anyone for that matter, that would make her happy it was her perspective that allowed her to generate that good feeling place. After a short while she entered into a relationship that was exciting and fun. One year after dating this gentleman she suggested a book to him that she knew he would enjoy and upon handing it to him the letter she had written two years prior fell out onto the floor. She picked it up and started to read it aloud and realized everything she had written had become her reality.

When you closely examine this story you will see the power you possess is the ability to get into a state of feeling that is preferable and whatever you give your attention to the universe will place in front of you. When you act on these results as best you can you will continue to be led to the next good thing, and on it goes. The more you stay in this state the more momentum you gain and the easier it becomes; this is basic physics. A simple understanding of how your inner guidance system works gives you control over your life's experience.

Take the time to write your story and allow it to unfold right before your very eyes.

Enjoy the Ride

If you take nothing else away from this book, know that your beliefs will never fail you. If you have a belief telling you that you cannot do something, built into that vibrating frequency are the cooperative components and the organizing principles that support the belief. Notice when you are in this state of doubt. When a particular desire arises, it is in that moment that a belief about the subject will generate a positive or negative reaction. If it makes you feel good, it is true; if it makes you feel bad, it is false. It really is as simple (and as complex) as that. You want to intellectualize and rationalize, even if it comes at the price of your good feelings. There is no universal truth other than love. There is no built-in meaning to anything other than the meaning you give it.

Who told you something was ultimately true? Was it a church, a person, someone you love and trust, a professor, a book? Nothing but love is universally true. Everything else is a matter of belief, and if you are aligned with your higher self, you will resonate with beliefs that are based in love.

Talk to your future self. In this present moment, you create your future reality with your imagination. If you consciously use your imagination to create an image of how you would like to feel while experiencing a particular event, you will generate good feelings that give rise to an emotion, resulting in an action that will lead you in the direction of what you imagined. If you act on it as best you can in the moment, it will head you in the direction of the image you imagined to be what you call your future self. Remember, hold no expectation, because you can't always intellectually understand how something is going to happen. But if you trust that the guiding principles will show you from moment to moment, and don't question it, you will enjoy the ride.

Is it ours to finish? Perhaps to end?
Why is it we came here?
Obsessive thought certainly can't be it;
And if we do figure it out how would we know?
After all, you can only discover the end
of something that has
ended and if it has ended there would be no one
to say nor no one
to listen
For this has not ended
Death certainly isn't the
End
We all die with something left to give,
therefore we never truly die
Just a mere shift in perspective
It must be; it never ends…
I will never know everything
I didn't come forth to finish
Certainly I won't figure it all out
Other than this moment
Life all is but a moment
So I shall experience it fully
From joy to sadness and everything in between
Done? Certainly not,
Just one with the meadow of feelings.

Notes

Notes

_____

_____

_____

_____

_____

_____

_____

_____

_____

_____

_____

_____

_____

Notes

_____

_____

_____

_____

_____

_____

_____

_____

_____

_____

_____

_____

_____

Notes

Notes

Notes

Notes

_____

_____

_____

_____

_____

_____

_____

_____

_____

_____

_____

_____

_____

Notes

Notes

_____

_____

_____

_____

_____

_____

_____

_____

_____

_____

_____

_____

Notes

_____

_____

_____

_____

_____

_____

_____

_____

_____

_____

_____

_____

_____

_____

Manufactured by Amazon.ca
Bolton, ON